The

The Art of Letting Go

From Separation in Love
to Fulfillment in Life

Carlino Giampolo

BANTAM BOOKS
NEW YORK · TORONTO · LONDON · SYDNEY · AUCKLAND

THE ART OF LETTING GO

*A Bantam Book / published by arrangement with
Carlino and Company*

PRINTING HISTORY

*Carlino and Company edition published 1988
Bantam edition / April 1990*

Library of Congress Cataloging-in-Publication Data

Giampolo, Carlino.
   The art of letting go / Carlino Giampolo.
      p.   cm.
   ISBN 0-553-34859-0
   1. Separation (Psychology) 2. Intimacy (Psychology) 3. Love.
4. Separation (Psychology)—Problems, exercises, etc. 5. Intimacy
(Psychology—Problems, exercises, etc. 6. Love—Problems,
exercises, etc. I. Title.
BF575.G7G5   1990
158'.2—dc20   89-17704
                                                          CIP

Published simultaneously in the United States and Canada

---

*Bantam Books are published by Bantam Books, a division of Bantam
Doubleday Dell Publishing Group, Inc. Its trademark, consisting of the
words "Bantam Books" and the portrayal of a rooster, is Registered in
U.S. Patent and Trademark Office and in other countries. Marca
Registrada. Bantam Books, 666 Fifth Avenue, New York, New York
10103.*

PRINTED IN THE UNITED STATES OF AMERICA

OPM   0 9 8 7 6 5 4 3 2 1

This book is dedicated to all those people who
are now in transition between the painful
breakup of an intimate relationship and the
joy of new beginnings. It is not meant as an
authoritative guide for living; rather, it represents
the sharing of the author's personal experience.
May the readers find a source of inspiration in the
pages that follow. It is hoped that by reading
the book and diligently doing the exercises, they
will develop the means necessary for their
own liberation.

My deepest gratitude to Bacco Mulligano
for help in the final writing of the text.

Contents

Introduction

Your pain is the breaking of the shell
that encloses your understanding.

Kahlil Gibran

Letting go of a loved one means moving from a period of
relative security into one which demands the redefining of an
individual's place and purpose in life. This is a painful yet
necessary process. The transition involves coming to terms
with two dimensions of challenge: the private reevaluation of
self and the mode of interacting with others. In the private
realm, an individual reflects upon the nature of personal
resources with which to live through the suffering involved in
separation. Once a healthy attitude toward the situation has
been established, the stage is set for embracing daily
experiences with the confidence and strength upon which a
meaningful life can be built.

The confusion which accompanies the pain of a separation is
one of the main impediments to resolving the dilemma of
people in the process of letting go of a loved one. This
confusion is, of course, characterized by unique circumstances

which relate to individual situations. The essence of the experience of separation is, however, universal. What follows on these pages is a journey through those areas of concern which all separations have in common. The reader's sincere reflection upon those realities which touch on all love separations can provide what is needed for every individual's liberation.

Exercise

Genuine desire is an indispensable groundwork for effective action. Affirm to yourself the desire to let go of the negativity surrounding your present situation. Give total commitment to this goal. Be clear-minded and determined in your purpose. Allow the words "I desire to let go" to become completely true for you.

Love

The falling out of lovers
is the renewing of love.
Robert Burton

Surround yourself with love. Though this may seem to you
the most impossible emotion to experience in the first stages
following a separation, it is to become your course of action
when you realize that love is the key to your control of self and
to the door that is opening toward your new reality. Love is
what brought you into your relationship and love is the power
that will lead you to the meaningful resolution of your situation.

This decision to love must first take effect with reference to
yourself and to the person from whom you are separating. You
must love yourself for those qualities which brought you into
the realm of that other person: your willingness to give of
yourself and to take the risk of being hurt. And to love the
other person in spite of the pain you are feeling is to allow that
person the same freedom you will both need in order to move
on. Love is a force that renews us and prepares us for tomorrow.
Hatred is a shackle that keeps us tied to the past. Drop the
shackles!

The one from whom you have separated will not soon be
forgotten, though great distances may separate the two of you.
Give the memory of that person the chance to help you by

8

insisting on remembering the beautiful experiences that united you. The painful ones which separated you will need no coaxing from the memory. Turn your anger into love. Take the qualities you found in the other person and develop them in yourself; use them as a way of better experiencing your love for all the others who are important in your life. After all, those were qualities which brought you into love and they are no less worthy today.

Love has no guilt and no boundaries. In fact, it has no definition. Yes, it is the force which takes us out of ourselves so that we may share ourselves with others. Yet it is also the force that leads us into ourselves, so that we may understand and prepare ourselves for the act of giving. You cannot resolve the bitterness and pain of the separation you are experiencing by continuing to dwell on these feelings. Come alive with the force which is the essence of life itself. You are leaving one relationship, one stop in your journey. There is still a path before you. Walk in love.

Exercise

Your love for the other person is now of a different nature. Daydream about the loved one and imagine yourself having a conversation in the framework of the new relationship. Create a loving conversation within this framework.

Spiritual Power

Oh! there is never sorrow of heart
That shall lack a timely end,
If but to God we turn, and ask
Of Him to be our friend!

William Wordsworth

Every human relationship leads us to a deeper consciousness of what lies beyond this earthly existence. All too frequently we forget this. Sometimes it takes an experience like the one you are now going through to enable you to place human events in their proper perspective. While it is true that much is to be gained by turning to other human beings in our time of need, we all feel the necessity of having recourse to a Power greater than ourselves. This Power is called God by some and for some it has no name, it simply is!

Pray to this Higher Force. Prayer means opening oneself to a channel of communication with the Power that lies beyond us. It means talking to that Power, giving thanks for our blessings, accepting our trials, admitting our weaknesses and asking for comfort and assurance. It is easy to see that the act of prayer, the act of openly coming to terms with ourselves by placing our doubts and confusion into the hands of some Force greater than ourselves, is part of the act of love itself. Thus, by praying we renew our confidence in love, which is the focal point of our human existence.

Clear your mind. Relax your body. Open yourself to yourself

and speak out from your heart to this Higher Force. This is prayer. You need not formulate into words what you wish to express. Your willingness to communicate your feelings is a language in itself. Then listen. This is meditation. The two acts of prayer and meditation should accompany one another. What you hear will be a form of silence. A divine silence. A comforting from afar.

Let the fruit of this act of communication be the sustenance of your daily life. You will begin to function more effectively in your world, the world which stares at you face to face, after you have undergone a painful separation, if you will just place some of the pain and confusion in the hands of that Power which is capable of assuming the suffering of all mankind. By binding yourself spiritually to that Power which binds all humans together, you reinforce your belief in your own ability to continue your quest for meaningful human relationships. The burdens of the daily life you are now facing will seem lighter for you. This will make you stronger for the work which lies ahead of you.

Exercise

Compose your own private prayer, asking for help in this troublesome moment in your life. In your prayer ask how you can become a channel of the Divine Peace, how you can bring this peace to others.

Beliefs

Believe that life is worth living,
and your belief will help create the fact.

William James

The measure of success you achieve in the process of letting go
will be determined to a great degree by your beliefs. They are the
framework upon which you build your future. Your beliefs are
the foundation for the shape your life will take from this point
onward. As such, they must be both solid and flexible. In other
words, you must always be sure that the beliefs which form the
base of your decisions and actions are strong enough to provide
support for the directions in which you are planning to go; and
yet at the same time, if these building blocks do not allow for
creative self-expansion, then progress will be beyond your reach.
By acknowledging which of your beliefs are beneficial to you
right now and which are not, you will achieve two goals: your
liberation from the pain of separation and the reconstruction of a
healthy base from which to conduct your future course of action.

It is during this time that you must assure yourself that the
foundations of your actions are secure and capable of permitting
growth and change. Remember that your beliefs predispose you
to action; they precede experience. Take this opportunity to
challenge your beliefs in all areas of your life. Hold on to those
convictions that enable you to maintain a sense of self-worth and
allow you to control your own destiny. Change those that you

know are preventing or slowing down your progress toward realizing your full potential as a human being.

Focus on where you are now. Analyze those beliefs of yours which have most to do with the process of letting go. Understand that if your beliefs in this process are centered around personal growth and healing, then your thoughts will coincide with these beliefs and will be guided by them. In this way you can actually empower yourself and bring about this growth and healing.

In order to have a more complete understanding of the fundamental beliefs which determine your actions, examine your beliefs with reference to each chapter of this book. By doing so you will be able to identify the underlying beliefs that are hurting yourself and others. Similarly, you will be assured of those basic principles that are essential to your well-being and to creating wholesome relationships with other people. And as you make the choice to build upon these positive attitudes, your potential for growth and happiness will expand.

Exercise

Be aware of those beliefs which you know are blocking your progress. Isolate them, examine them carefully, and then change them. Strengthen those beliefs which have contributed most in the past to your personal growth and make them continue to work for you.

Forgiveness

To err is human, to forgive divine.

Alexander Pope

The road on which you are traveling is not an easy one. Why clutter it with more obstacles than it already presents to you? Tear down the stumbling block of resentment and cast it aside. Forgive! Clear the path and get on with your journey.

It is unrealistic to place all the blame for the events that have led to your separation on the other person. This you already know. And by insisting on continuing your resentment even for those acts which are clearly the fault of the other, you only persist in creating an even more difficult situation for yourself. What good can come from dredging up all of the negative aspects of the other person's character? None. And whether you are willing to admit it or not, the relationship which the two of you formed together was made possible first and foremost by those characteristics which you have in common.

To forgive is to release from blame. You should remember that your act of forgiving, of removing the blame, should be two-fold: to forgive the other person and to also forgive yourself.

Forgive the other person, so that you may both be able to see the world clearly in the present tense. Blame, like hatred, keeps you a prisoner of the past. You have your version of that past. The other person has another version. You both have done what you were able to do with the resources at your disposal. That is all history. Close that book!

Forgive yourself for any shortcomings in your part of the relationship. This is one of the most important keys to self-respect. Release yourself from guilt. Pardon yourself as you pardon the other person. Just as you were capable of committing some of the errors that led to the decline of the relationship, you are also worthy of forgiveness. This pardon may or may not come from the other person. Most importantly it must come from you. You are in a position now where you need to concentrate most of your energies in the direction of rebuilding that confidence which is the first step to rebuilding your life.

Your future relationships, starting from today, will bear the stamp of your self-respect as it is today. By eliminating that which is of no value to you, namely the useless blame of yourself or others, you are ready to face the future now.

Exercise

Forgive the one who may be causing you pain. If you think that you are partly or wholly at fault for what has happened, forgive yourself. Daydream about being in the other person's presence, asking to be forgiven and in turn forgiving.

Trust

Better trust all, and be deceived
And weep that trust and that deceiving,
Than doubt one heart that if believed
Had blessed one's life with true believing.

Frances Anne Kemble

Begin now to open yourself to others. Do not put this off.
Trust in the world, though it may seem hostile. This will be
perhaps one of the most difficult tasks for you to accomplish in
the weeks and months that lie ahead of you. Embrace the task
willingly, using as your primary tool the awareness you have
of the good you have received from all those who love you.

Your initial response to a painful separation may include an
intense reluctance to place your trust in someone once again.
You can overcome this hesitation by concentrating on the
relationship between the various forms of love and affection
which surround us in our lives. Just as you can count on the
tenderness and sincerity of some friends and family members,
you can count on the possibility of this love from others as well.
To transfer the negative feelings which you may associate with
the relationship you are ending to the world at large is unrealistic.

Every situation is unique. Every person is unique. Think of
how you first met one of your good friends, perhaps years ago,
quite by accident. Think of how this friendship grew stronger
through the years, battling all adversity. You and that one
person have maintained the love of friendship through your

trust in one another. Perhaps other friendships were not so successful. In the same way you must open yourself to the possibility of entering into an intimate relationship which will go beyond the one which you have just left. Do not go out in haste in search of such a relationship. But do not shut yourself off from the possibility of growing into a close human bond once again.

In order to prepare yourself for this stage of opening up to new relationships, trust in yourself. Be honest with yourself.

Those qualities which are a permanent part of your character and which have led you into meaningful interactions with all those you have ever loved and who have loved you did not suddenly vanish when this relationship came to an end. Your ability to open up to others has not disappeared. Your potential for loving, in spite of the risks involved, always was and still is the main source of your faith in life. Renew this faith by trusting the world once again. Renew your life by maintaining trust in yourself.

Exercise

On one piece of paper, write down the positive features of a person whom you have recently met. On another paper, write down the negative ones. Then tear up the negative list. Use the positive list as the basis for getting to know that person better.

Self-Image

The great mystery is not that we should have
been thrown down here at random between
the profusion of matter and that of the stars;
it is that from our very prison we should draw,
from our own selves, images powerful enough
to deny our nothingness.

André Malraux

The way in which you see yourself and your relationship to
the world around you is the core of the image you convey to
your fellow human beings, and lies at the center of the interactions which take place between you and them. Before you
can hope to succeed in achieving harmony with the world, you
must first confront the task of understanding yourself. This is,
of course, an on-going process, one in which you have been
constantly involved throughout your life. During this period of
your separation from a loved one, however, it is absolutely
essential that you concentrate on the importance of self-
knowledge. The primary energies necessary for your victory
over this present crisis can come only from you.

Maintain your self-respect and your sense of self-worth. Your
positive qualities and achievements in life to this point have
not suddenly dropped out of existence. The awareness you
have of your own capacity for working through difficult
situations is a priceless treasure at this time. Use it to its fullest
advantage. It is a power which you have developed slowly and
patiently through many seemingly insurmountable dilemmas,

and to lose sight of it now would be to set up a dangerous stumbling block in your life. Know that you are strong enough to make it through this stressful time without losing any of your self-esteem.

It is true that predicaments like the one you are now experiencing are a tremendous drain on the personal resources needed in life to achieve and maintain well-being. Your storehouse of potentials, however, is not a shallow pool. By taking inventory of your strongest qualities and looking at them honestly, you will be able to use what you see in your total self-image as the means by which to get back to the business of your life, your future. There are no failures, only outcomes. At this moment you are actually in the middle of the process of determining the outcome of the separation with which you are now confronted.

Work with the thoughts and beliefs that empower you. You are the only one who can filter out the useless forces from your own conception of yourself, forces such as guilt and self-blame. By concentrating on the best of the elements which make up your total image of yourself, you will be able to come through this experience complete and prepared for your own growth and development.

Exercise

Evaluate yourself. Concentrate on your good qualities and strong points. Make a list of your personal assets and reflect on them. Make this an on-going process.

Responsibility

There is no duty we so much underrate
as the duty of being happy.

Robert Louis Stevenson

You are responsible for your world. At every major turn of
events, you must be accountable for the way in which you are
conducting your life. Now that you are in the process of facing
the reality of separation from a loved one, you are choosing
the direction which the rest of your life will take. And, of course,
you hold yourself responsible for the choices you make in life.
Your decision to enter into a relationship was an indication of
your confidence in life. This same confidence must be your
guiding force now as you assess your present situation. You
have to answer only to yourself, both for what has already taken
place in your life and for what course you choose for meeting
the terms of your future growth.

To look at the events of your life as some network of outside
forces acting upon you is to lose sight of the primary role which
you play in the development of your own destiny. Always be
conscious of the responsibility you must assume for the way
things develop around you. This consciousness is the corner-
stone of a mature approach to reality.

Your ego is, in and of itself, a positive force. It represents
an essential part of your instinct to protect yourself, thus allowing

you to confront life's challenges effectively. However, like any positive force taken to extremes, an exaggeration of your ego can only lead you to defeat. Your responsibility to yourself should not be confused with an unbending impulse to protect your own belief system at all costs. The image which you have of yourself has been tested over and again by you. It is firmly in place. Clearly it is your responsibility to maintain the powers which are already yours and to use them for developing new ones. This must be done with a clear mind and in a spirit of humility.

Your own existence is only one life force in conjunction with the rest of humanity. Your actions have a direct effect not only on you but on everyone with whom you come into contact. Life is a process of interdependence. At every step in the formation of this new world which you are creating, you must look at your decisions and actions with an honest sense of perspective. By constantly holding yourself accountable for the way in which you personally mesh with the total fabric of life, you will assure yourself of the harmony which leads to growth.

Exercise

Believe and acknowledge to yourself that you alone are responsible for what happens to you. Repeat this affirmation over and over again: "I am the captain of my own ship. I am in charge of my life. I am not a creature of circumstances."

Acceptance

I accept the universe!

Margaret Fuller

Take hold of yourself and accept yourself for what you are now. Avoid the natural tendency toward trying to imagine the past as it could have been. Such thinking is a trap which can only immobilize you. What really happened is already clear to you. What could have been is nonexistent.

It is important that you develop now a willingness to see things as they really are. In order to accomplish this, it will be necessary to break down any barriers which may be blocking a clear perception of the present situation. These barriers were originally constructed by you, in an attempt to camouflage painful aspects of the separation. Know that in order to let go of your pain, you will have to acknowledge and accept its existence. And then you will need to accept two things: the way in which this situation relates to the person from whom you are separating and your interpretation of how this difficult situation affects you and the other person.

You can see that it is not possible, nor is it desirable, to try to change the other person. To attempt changing another is a frustrating and useless approach to the resolution of your dilemma. Show respect for the one whom you are leaving.

Accept the pain of your present experience and explore all the positive outcomes of this major change in both of your lives. Accept the fact that the other person is also in the process of moving toward the creation of a new and meaningful life. This acceptance will provide you with the space and energy you will need in going forward with your own life.

Come to terms with yourself and be willing to enter into the flow of moving toward the realization of your own potential. Self-acceptance is of the utmost importance at this time. You have found within yourself the capability of accepting the pain of the present reality. You are equally capable of appreciating the satisfaction which awaits you as you gain complete acceptance of yourself.

Exercise

Make the following affirmation to yourself repeatedly: "I accept those things in my life which I know I cannot change. I accept, as well, my own ability to move on toward the accomplishment of what I know I can achieve."

Feelings

The most important part of man's existence, that part where he most truly lives and is aware of living, lies entirely within the domain of personal feeling.

Joyce Cary

Your feelings represent the way in which you react to your perception of the world around you. As such, they are fundamental indicators of what you understand to be the truth. At this time, it is especially important that you see your situation as realistically as possible. You will first have to acknowledge your feelings in order to be able to free yourself from those negative feelings which are standing in your way.

Denial is usually the first response to a breakup. Pretending that the separation is not really happening, however, only delays the process of letting go to which you have committed yourself. Try to work through this feeling by not attempting to expect more than the reality of the situation in which you find yourself. Once you rid yourself of denial and accept the breakup of the relationship, you can truly begin the process of letting go.

Anxiety is also a natural reaction to the pain of separation. It is the feeling of uncertainty about the future and it can be real or imaginary. But your anxiety can be alleviated once you accept the fact that you are capable of overcoming the difficulties of a separation one step at a time. The fear of not being able to cope is resolved through an honest acceptance of the powers which you know are yours.

In letting go, let go of your anger as well and heal your emotional wounds. Expressing anger is a healthy response to a stressful situation, as long as it is expressed in an appropriate manner. But overreacting is as unhealthy as not reacting at all. Because you feel yourself to be hurt, the temptation may exist to hurt the other person. Rise above this feeling by being in total control of your situation. Express your anger with kindness, openness and honesty.

Unwarranted guilt is one of the most counterproductive of human feelings. If you have done something which you know was wrong, real guilt should lead you to seek forgiveness. But even then, you cannot dwell upon feelings of guilt without rendering yourself passive. And unfounded guilt is an even more destructive path. During these initial stages of your separation, reexamine your belief system. Be kind to yourself and ask what is best for you. Realize that it is never possible to meet all the expectations another person has of you. There will always be the feeling that you could have done more. Transfer this feeling into the opposite of negative guilt: positive constructive action. You will be a better person.

Do the same with any negative feelings which you encounter during this painful time. Confront them openly and with courage, transforming them into the positive energies which will lead you through all the difficulties of letting go.

Exercise

Be honest with yourself about your feelings. Then express any painful feeling you may have to the person from whom you are separating. This may be done in person, in writing (whether you mail it or not), or in an imaginary way.

Learning

All experience is an arch to build upon.

Henry Brooks Adams

See your present crisis for what it really is. You are not stuck in the middle of an incomprehensible situation. What is happening to you now is an integral part of the continuity of learning. The knowledge which you are gaining about yourself and others at this time will serve as the groundwork of your future decisions and actions. While some learning situations are joyous in nature, others are characterized by pain and suffering. The anguish which you are feeling now represents a necessary stage in your progress. It is true that you must seek to overcome your pain as soon as possible. You realize, however, that you can only go beyond your present suffering by recognizing its existence and actually living through it. You have at your disposal already the sum of painful situations which you have come through successfully. Learning experiences build upon one another. You are now acquiring an even greater ability to cope with adversity. The learning process is a constant form of accomplishment.

Things happen for a reason and a purpose. The events of your life are not isolated fragments. Reflect on the connections between this phase of your experience and the other challenging periods which have strengthened you to this point. This particular step in your life represents the gaining of new information to be used in your evolution as an individual and as a successful participant in society. And you realize that you are not alone in your experiences. The people with whom you will want to formulate new relationships in the near future will also have lived through similar conditions.

The open acceptance of all dimensions of learning leads to the discovery of truth. Each difficulty that you are now confronting represents a facet of your development of self-knowledge. You are getting to know yourself better by means of your separation from a loved one. Confront yourself. Look upon this phase of your life as one of the most valuable growth experiences ever presented to you. Learning and growth go hand in hand. You are truly in the process of coming to grips with yourself.

Your self-knowledge is the basis of your interaction with others. Look at yourself honestly at this time, recognizing your strengths as well as your weaknesses. The more realistic you are in your self-evaluation, the more prepared you will be for discovering your potential to share with others what you have learned in life.

Exercise

Ask yourself what you have learned from your association with the other person. Make a list of those learning experiences which you know will be useful to you now and in the near future.

Thoughts

Human thought is the process by which
human ends are ultimately answered.

Daniel Webster

Your thoughts are one of the principal sources of your power to
control your own destiny. There are some important aspects of
the thought process with which you are probably already familiar.
You may know that your thoughts are capable of altering bodily
functions. In some instances, in the martial arts, for example, a
change in thoughts can bring about a change in actual physical
power. In a similar manner, the way in which you deal with your
thoughts during this time of separation can determine the measure
of success you will have in working through your conflict.

Think your thoughts out to the very end and you will see that
your painful situation is not so extreme as you had perhaps
believed. Realize that past situations in which you have found
yourself cannot be changed; your perception of these experiences,
however, is within your control. You have within you the capacity
for changing any negative thoughts into positive ones.

By working with each negative thought individually, you will
begin to understand your ability to master your own thought
processes. Two thoughts cannot occupy the same space in
consciousness. And it takes several seconds after a thought arises
in the brain to identify the thought context to which it belongs, to

decide to change it, and to make that change. Blocking or obstructing any negative thought, you understand, is only self-defeating. Even the most negative thoughts are ultimately subject to the form which you give to them. You will believe only what you choose to believe, what you tell yourself to believe.

Of course you are attempting, as much as possible, during this difficult period, not to dwell on thoughts about the other person. And you should be trying as well to give less attention to past negative thoughts. But you also realize that it is your responsibility to yourself to challenge any unpleasant thought when it rises up before you, so as to clear the way for a healthier thought process. After thinking a negative thought concerning your breakup and working through that thought, let it be clear to you that the outcome of that thought will be positive because of your will to make it so. Then make your next thought this: "I desire to let go." By doing so, you will confirm your original goal to deal with all the necessary stages of this painful time in your life. And you will be prepared to master and shape the thoughts which accompany you in this process of arriving at a positive outcome to your separation.

Exercise

Be cognizant of your thoughts at all times and use your power to change negative thoughts concerning your breakup into positive ones.

Friends

Friendship is composed of a single soul
inhabiting two bodies.

Aristotle

The gift of friendship ranks among the greatest blessings of
this life. It is a force which consistently proves its own validity
and virtue through good times as well as bad. Your friends are
those who take joy in your happiness, as you do in theirs.
Similarly, you suffer willingly for one another during times of
distress. Just as your friends are here now to stand beside you in
your difficulty, they are also very anxious to see you move on
through this period of stress. They wish to share with you in the
positive outcome which you are going to make of this situation.

Consider some of the ways in which your friends can help
you through this difficult phase of your life. One of the most
useful means of working out your present dilemma is the
process of verbalization. Talk openly and honestly with your
friends about your present crisis, just as you encourage them to
do when life has presented them with some obstacle. This will
allow you to release those pent-up frustrations which can only
hold back your liberation from the pain you are experiencing.
Who can place a value on the feedback provided by conversa-
tions with a friend?

Select the friend or friends in whom you wish to confide at

this time with intelligence and fairness. To choose someone who is a close friend both to you and to the person from whom you are separating could result in creating more stress for all three of you, since that friend would be forced to take sides. Your goal at this moment is to release yourself and others from as much suffering as possible; so it would be wise for you to place your trust now in a friend whose loyalty is dedicated to you.

You may feel that the nature of your crisis is such that even your best friends cannot succeed in helping you to unravel completely the knot of emotions you are now living through. Seeking professional assistance for your problems can be an indication of a realistic understanding of the complex nature of your difficulties. In no way does it represent a betrayal of friendship on your part. In fact, if you choose this course of action, you can discuss it freely with close friends.

Your true friends will gladly bear with you, no matter what path you choose for arriving at the positive outcome toward which you are now headed. And when you arrive there, your joy will be theirs as well.

Exercise

Make a commitment now to discuss your problems, thoughts and sentiments candidly and honestly with a trusted friend or counselor.

Activity

Whether you'll try for the goal that's afar
Or be contented to stay just where you are.
Take it or leave. Here's something to do,
Just think it over. It's all up to you!
                                Elizabeth Barrett Browning

   The severe stress of a separation tends to immobilize the
people involved and it is for this reason that your ability to
spring back to action is of the utmost significance at this time.
Meet your present crisis with a sense of vigor and liveliness.
These are the perfect antidotes to the sluggishness that comes
with depression and confusion. The sooner you begin to engage
in positive and constructive action, the sooner you will feel the
healing process moving within you.
   Mental and physical activities are of equal importance in
restoring yourself to a healthy and productive state. The mind
and body work as a unit in the achievement of the vitality
necessary for overcoming inertia. Return quickly to the
activities in both of these realms that give you pleasure and
increase your feelings of strength and purpose. By immersing
yourself in the things which intensify your awareness of the
forward thrust of life, you will place yourself back on the path
of the productive future which lies ahead of you.
   Challenge yourself as well to become involved in an activity
which you have never before attempted. Set this new horizon
for yourself now, by taking the first steps in accomplishing a

goal which you had perhaps thought about in the past, without ever actually confronting it face to face. Approach this activity with total self-confidence. Be resilient. Bend with the new experience, accepting all its facets, its possibilities. Move into this adventure with passion and trust.

Take up an activity which will put you at risk. What will you learn or accomplish without risk? You know that taking a chance at something is the only real way of truly coming to grips with it. Love itself takes risks as part of its natural course. Engage yourself in a risk-taking situation with confidence in your heart. Grow from the experience, moving forward at all times from where you are now. Make your trust in life active.

Embrace openly another of life's most rewarding actions, that of extending yourself to someone else, doing good for someone else. The energies which flow between you and the person to whom you reach out are as beneficial to you as they are to the other person. Your life is ultimately the total of your actions and, more importantly, of your interactions with others. Giving of yourself places you into active participation in life. Sharing with others strengthens your own character, keeping you firmly grounded in your path toward progress.

Exercise

Select one mental activity and one physical activity in which you have always wanted to become involved, and take immediate steps to put these two desires into action.

Change of Scenery

The soul of a journey is liberty, perfect
liberty, to think, feel, do just as one pleases.
We go a journey chiefly to be free of all
impediments and of all inconveniences; to
leave ourselves behind.

William Hazlitt

   Much of the negative energy involved in a separation from a
loved one comes to be associated with the physical locales in
which the relationship to that person grew and then disinte-
grated. This is a feeling which is all too familiar to anyone who
is experiencing the pain of separation. It is natural for you to
identify certain places with the emotions connected to
experiences you have lived through in those places. And it is
just as natural for you to wish to remove yourself from those
surroundings, so as to be distanced from settings which now
seem to work against you as you attempt to remake your life.
Take the opportunity to give yourself a change of scenery, since
the effect of such a change is one of refreshment and inspiration.
   As soon as possible, you might begin to take small trips,
perhaps away from the town or city in which you live. Traveling
with a friend can be an excellent way of removing yourself from
troublesome contexts and of engaging in the undisturbed
company of someone with whom you enjoy spending time.
Or you may choose to travel on your own. Such an experience
has the benefit of placing you in a situation where you can reach
out to new acquaintances or take advantage of peaceful solitary

meditation in a setting which is free from all associations.

These small journeys away from your immediate context are beneficial as a needed temporary relief from a stressful situation. Most importantly, however, you know that you are in the process of developing a new outlook with which to readjust to the setting in which you live permanently. The ultimate value of what you experience during your travels will have to be incorporated into your life, once you have returned to your familiar setting. The true benefit derived from travel has to do with the development of your ability for discovery. In your journeys you are constantly surrounded with a sense of newness and vitality. Learn to appreciate the excitement associated with discovery, and look upon this stimulation as an ongoing experience. Carry this excitement home with you.

Enjoy the place in which you find yourself. It is within your potential to reinterpret the reality in which you live. You are now challenging yourself to discover the new and positive dimensions of the setting in which you are restructuring your life.

Exercise

Even if it is only for a day, get away from your usual locale. Take a long or short trip somewhere. Visit a near or far place that you have always wanted to see. Let a change of scenery allow you to take your mind away from your problems.

Laughter

We are all here for a spell;
get all the good laughs you can.

Will Rogers

The joy of living is as much within your grasp now as it ever
was. Remember this and reach out at this time toward the
delightful things which life has to offer. The transition in which
you now find yourself is a movement toward the discovery of
the joy of new beginnings. Assert your right to take pleasure
in the people and situations which bring you happiness. Look
at the light side of your circumstances. Have the courage to
laugh.

Life has shown you countless times the immeasurable value
of laughter. You know that once you are able to talk about an
unfortunate experience, it is under your control; and once you
can laugh at it, you have conquered it. Even your most serious
past mistakes contain some aspect of humor. Recognize that
this is true. When you succeed in laughing at yourself for your
own misfortunes, you put into motion a new set of positive
thought patterns and open yourself once again to the
recognition of your potential for happiness. Thus, it is within
your power to lift the cloud of negativity which causes one to
forget that life is to be enjoyed.

Even on the physical level, laughter is known to calm and
soothe the body and to relieve it from pain. In a similar way,

it brightens the entire spirit and awakens it to an awareness of the beauty of life. Why continue to dwell in the world of bitterness, when laughter opens the door to delight? Just as you have lived many happy and humorous experiences in past relationships, it is now time to create new situations in which you can be brought back into contact with the cheerfulness of life. Such contact should be a daily occurrence. It is only when we see the comical side of so many of our daily experiences and treat them in a lighthearted manner that we can relax to the point of being comfortable with ourselves and with those around us.

Just as you have faced your pain and confusion openly during this separation, you should live up to your capacity for being joyful as well. Open yourself to the humorous dimension of life. It surrounds you and invites you at every turn. Share your amusement and your willingness to laugh with others and the joy you impart to them will return to you and strengthen you.

Exercise

Spend more time with those friends with whom you find it easy to laugh and joke. Involve yourself in activities you know will entertain you: see a funny film, read a humorous book.

The Future

I shall walk eager still for what Life holds
Although it seems the hard road will not end—
One never knows the beauty round the bend!

Anna Blake Mezquida

With every form of adversity comes the seed of an equal or greater benefit. Look upon your future as the bright outcome of the storm you are living through during this time of your separation. Most importantly, you must believe in the positive value of this outcome, which will perhaps require a change in your perspective. If you keep in mind the idea that all things happen for a reason and a purpose, it will be easier for you to create out of your future a positive result of your painful experience.

The future will be happier. Make this your guiding principle. Meditate upon it; listen to the bright messages of things to come. Understand that if you have been capable of getting through the chaos of this separation, you are that much more prepared to be the master of what lies ahead of you. Think in these terms. Give yourself credit for the courage with which you are meeting your present circumstances and accept the fact that this very positive quality of yours is the springboard toward a positive future.

The future is the greatest source of inspiration that you have. It represents an entire world of possibilities. These possibilities are clearly within your reach only if you will develop now the proper attitude toward your own future potentials. Make an attempt to imagine and visualize this future. Set goals for yourself which are stepping stones in the direction of that bright future as you imagine it. Before you now lies the greatest opportunity of all: the chance to realize your own growth and development to its maximum. Think of the experience of your separation as the first stage in the movement toward a better future life for yourself and for those whom you will encounter as you weave the texture of things as they are to be. You are now one step higher in the understanding of human relationships. And that understanding, without a doubt, is the most significant of all in the creation of a meaningful and successful future.

The optimism which is necessary in order to make things happen in your favor lies entirely within your grasp. Your whole future depends upon the attitude with which you approach it. Make that attitude the most positive one imaginable. Remember that your future is everything and that you have the power to make it as bright as you wish.

Exercise

Relax. Close your eyes. Picture a bright future for yourself. Now imagine some goal that you know can be obtained in a very short time and review in your mind what you will do to attain it.

Communication

Self-expression must pass into communication
for its fulfillment.

Helen Hull

The process of letting go is naturally one of deep introspection, of looking into yourself in order to understand yourself better. This self-examination, however, should be understood as a preliminary step toward the act of conveying to others, in the clearest manner possible, your thoughts and feelings concerning your present state and your plans for the future. Take advantage of your ability to see your own situation realistically; use this ability as a means of preparing yourself for as open a dialogue as possible with the other person. As you gain knowledge and strength in your determination to let go, you gain the means for communicating to your former partner your intention to do so and the steps you plan to take in doing it.

If the channels of communication between you and the other person are already open, you may want to discuss together some of the contents of this book and what it is you are learning from it. This could enable both of you to have a clearer understanding of each other's position in this difficult situation and could serve as a bridge between you for the interchange of ideas and feelings.

If such is not the case, then you should seek to find the most sincere means of communication possible for the expression of your thoughts to the other person. This may take the form of a personal visit; or you may have to achieve this important step by means of a telephone call or a letter.

Whatever manner you find best for reaching out to the other person, always keep in mind the necessity for doing so. Communication removes the uncertainty which all too often clouds the reality of a separation. It is this uncertainty which prolongs a painful situation and prevents those who are separating from coming to grips with the decisions which will be necessary for meeting the serious challenges presented by separation.

Communication helps you to become more committed to your original goal of wanting to let go. Once you have conveyed openly and honestly to the other person what your intentions are, your energies will be directed outward and you will begin to feel a sense of freedom from built-up negative emotions. Your goal is to move forward, and in order to do this you will have to place yourself in a position of being able to communicate with the rest of the world. Your communication with the person from whom you are separating is an invaluable step in this direction.

Exercise

In a manner that is best for you—in person, by telephone or by letter—communicate to the person from whom you are separating your willingness to let go.

Music

Music is the universal language of mankind.

Henry Wadsworth Longfellow

One of the purest forms for the expression of ideas and emotions is music. This is a gift which is always at your disposal. During this time of separation, it can serve as a means of relaxation and inspiration. By choosing wisely the kind of music with which you surround yourself, you can in many ways prepare for the challenges which await you in this transformation you are undergoing.

Choose music to listen to which will create for you an oasis of peace in which you can meditate on the rhythms of life and thus strengthen yourself. The harp and the flute, for example, are instruments whose music is conducive to such a state of relaxation. Meditative music helps us to suspend our worries and to replenish the peaceful energies which are necessary for emotional balance. In this period you owe it to yourself to achieve such a balance, so that you will be able to confront your future with a sense of calm reassurance.

In addition to listening to live or recorded music which will provide for you a healthy frame of mind, you have within you a wealth of personal musical experiences. From your memory you can draw on many forms of music which bring about in you a positive effect. You can bring to life within yourself melodies which remove you from your feelings of solitude or produce in you good feelings about yourself and about the world in which you live. Enjoy these personal musical delights by singing or humming them to yourself. By doing so, you will appreciate more thoroughly the continuity which music has had in your life and you will allow yourself to reap more abundantly its benefits.

One of music's most important dimensions is the communication that it creates among people. Music brings people together. Go to the places where music puts you in happy contact with others. In the public sphere, dance is the counterpart to music. Dance turns the spiritual quality of music into the physical. Dance to the music.

Allow music to work its full powers upon you at this time. Take advantage of its potential for healing wounds and creating a bridge for interpersonal communication. What you are truly seeking now is harmony within yourself and between you and the rest of the world. Music is one of the most beautiful expressions of this harmony.

Exercise

Be aware of the music that surrounds you in your daily life. Sing to yourself or listen to music which inspires you toward positive feelings and places you in harmony with the world around you.

Autosuggestion

Every day, in every way,
I am getting better and better.

Émile Coué

Your imagination is certainly among the most profound of your personal resources. The ability to create images, to visualize, is what enables you to link together the subconscious and conscious dimensions of your thoughts. That which you choose to visualize or imagine as your reality will condition, to a great degree, the way in which your reality will actually occur. So much of the real outcome of this separation you are experiencing will depend upon the way in which you envision that outcome. The power to shape reality is yours; and it begins with your power to visualize your life as you know it ought to be.

The suggestions you make to yourself, by means of what you visualize on the subconscious level, are the building blocks for your real behavior. This is because the human mind is constantly forming new connections between subconscious and conscious life. Ask yourself: What is my image of the positive resolution of my situation? How would I feel if this resolution had actually been realized? What would my day be like today? Get into the habit of visualizing the details of your new life as you see them in your mind's eye. Be constantly aware that the two levels of reality, the subconscious and the conscious, flow easily into one another. This awareness is what will enable you to transform your thoughts into actions.

Once you have accepted the intimate connection between what is suggested by the mind and what is actually done, begin immediately to act as though the resolution of your difficulties had already occurred. There are virtually no limits to what can be accomplished when you begin to live out the images which you have created for yourself. Past habits which impeded your total development can be broken. New and positive behavior can be visualized and lived out. Within a matter of days you can bring to reality the first stage of your liberation from suffering as you visualize it. In a few weeks you will be well on your way to living out completely the reality you have suggested to yourself.

The recognition of your desire to let go is something you have already accomplished. Now your expectations and the genuine belief that you can achieve the goal of letting go will clarify your vision of the successful realization of that goal. This vision, in turn, must come to fruition by means of your ability to act it out in real life. It is your vision of your positive reality. Begin to live it.

Exercise

With your own method, place yourself in a state of relaxation. Creatively visualize the conditions of your new situation; you have already liberated yourself from your suffering. Visualize the positive steps you are taking in the creation of your new life.

Strength

The turning point in the process of growing up is when you discover the core of strength within you that survives all hurt.

Max Lerner

Now that you have made the decision to let go, be constantly aware that you have within you the strength to carry out that decision in such a way that what lies ahead of you can only lead to success. Remember that it was your own fortitude which allowed you to face honestly the need for this separation. And your own inner resources provided you with the capacity for going through with the only course of action which could lead you to a meaningful direction for your life. You are now embarking on a time in your life when you will need to make other very difficult decisions. Be convinced that the same inner strength which has brought you this far will continue to enable you to take charge of your life.

It is natural for you to seek the help of loved ones and friends during this trying period. Such help, when offered, should be accepted and utilized by you with a sense of appreciation and love. Keep in mind, however, that the burden ultimately lies on your own shoulders and that you are indeed strong enough to bear this weight with a positive attitude; and that, if necessary, you can stand alone in doing it. Your task is to heal your wounds now so that you will be prepared to contribute to your own growth and development and, in turn, to that of others.

Continue to reevaluate your decisions as you work through each phase of this breakup. At each step, have the courage to do what is best for you. Be strong-minded and resilient in your efforts to let go. Every decision you make during this time should reflect your awareness of your own power to succeed. Let no one intimidate you. With perseverance you will see your way through all the decisions necessary for getting you back to your normal self.

By drawing upon the power which you have worked so hard at developing, you will be able to meet any eventuality caused by this separation. Be steadfast in your determination to avoid playing the role of victim or martyr. Think of the worst possible scenario in connection with this breakup. Is it that bad? Surely not. The most difficult scenario, that of the process of deciding to let go, is one which you have already mastered because of your inner strength. That same strength is still yours for meeting every challenge that stands before you. Continue to be firm in your decision. Walk forward courageously.

Exercise

Imagine the worst possible scenario that may occur because of your separation. Then realize that no matter how bad that situation may seem to be, you have the strength necessary to see it through to a successful conclusion.

Giving

When I give I give myself.

Walt Whitman

At this time, it is natural for you to be thinking about all that you have given to that person from whom you are now separating. Not only is this natural; it is necessary, in order for you to establish a better understanding of your potential for future growth. To dwell upon the idea that you gave too much or too little, however, is counterproductive and will keep you tied to the past. You must be able to see the act of giving as being intimately connected to that which you receive in your life experiences.

In order to have a clearer knowledge of the relationship between giving and receiving, you will have to consider what your motivation was in giving something in the first place. Where you feel pain or resentment for what you have given, the guiding force behind the giving was itself negative. It was based upon a calculation of what you expected to receive in return. The benefits of love cannot be calculated. Where you feel genuine joy for having given, it is because your giving was really a sharing of yourself. Giving as sharing of oneself is the very foundation of love.

Your mind should be focused on the spiritual sharing which was the core of your relationship. This is not to say that the material concerns involved in this separation are not important. They are; but they are secondary to your development as a person capable of sharing a life with someone else. And you should treat them as such. If there must be a division of shared material possessions, then go about making this division with a sense of fairness and love.

When you give freely, you are always the recipient. Keep this idea foremost in your mind. As you examine your past, try to recognize the occasions when your open sharing of yourself was the source of your joy and of your sense of freedom. Concentrate upon the experiences in which the love you received was the pure counterpart of the love you gave.

This period of separation affords you the opportunity to learn more about yourself and your potential for giving. Carry the fruits of the experiences you shared in the relationship into your present life. Practice freely the act of giving and of seeing this giving as a sharing of yourself. Life itself is the greatest giver of all. By realizing this, you will be at peace with yourself and capable of giving back to life your greatest gift—yourself.

Exercise

Examine clearly all aspects of giving and receiving which characterized your relationship. Recognize any problems in this area which still exist between you and the person from whom you are separating; resolve these problems with love and fairness.

Viewpoint

Each man sees what he carries in his heart.

Johann Wolfgang von Goethe

The way in which you view your present situation in its relation to the rest of your life is all important. Look upon this period of your experience as an opportunity for growth. Every moment of your life, in fact, represents such an opportunity, as long as you are willing to see it as such.

What separates success from failure is the way in which we perceive the possibilities inherent in all of life's circumstances. Even in your sorrow you can find joy if your viewpoint in reference to that sorrow allows you to do so. Your joy will consist of the understanding that sorrow has served to strengthen you for the future which you have already begun to live out.

The root of continued pain lies frequently in an error of perception. It lies in the refusal to see the positive aspects of every human act. A healthy outlook on even the most negative experience eliminates frustration and opens the way toward the kind of self-image which can direct any chain of events to a successful conclusion. How often have you worried about things that never came to pass?

This was wasted energy; for even when what seemed insurmountable did come your way, you were more than prepared to live through your difficulties with a sense of accomplishment and strength. Your present situation is a perfect example of this ability of yours.

Shifting your perspective does not imply a dilution of your value system. On the contrary, changes in point of view from one of life's encounters to the next serve as a way of reinforcing the total structure of the accumulated values which guide your actions every day. Maintain that high level of esteem in which you originally held this relationship which is now ending. It was the circumstances alone which prevented its continued development.

Love itself is still at the top of your hierarchy of values. And this love can be understood in new ways, if you will permit yourself to look upon the nature of love in its myriad of forms. These include the desire to help make life better for your fellow human beings and the commitment to pursuing spiritual power and knowledge, especially self-knowledge.

You cannot change the events of your past. What you can change is the way in which you view the significance of these events and the place they occupy in the total mosaic of your existence. See them for what they really are, and build around them in such a way that the complete picture of this phase of your experience is in keeping with your ultimate vision of life.

Exercise

Begin now to develop a positive viewpoint toward the separation which you are undergoing. Make this viewpoint a daily guiding force in your pattern of developing those values which you hold highest in life.

Thinking

Reading furnishes our mind with
materials of knowledge;
it is thinking that makes what we read ours.

John Locke

In the process of thinking we are as much involved in
generating new choices for ourselves as we are in
gathering information based on past experiences. The
recognition of this power is what permits us to enlarge our
vision of the world and of our place within it. And we can
change our understanding of the world by changing the
way we think.

During this period of transition it is important for you
to see that good thinking is controlled thinking. Simply
shifting from one emotion to another can only bring
confusion. Think first, sort out your thoughts; and then
give close attention to each of your emotions in order to
determine which are appropriate and which are not. In this
way, you control your emotions; they do not control you.

All of us have many beliefs and attitudes which we
ourselves have already developed or which we have simply
accepted as being absolute. Some of these fundamental
beliefs are essential, in order for us to maintain a healthy
sense of equilibrium within society. It should be clear,
however, that some of our self-made or unquestioned

notions may be blocking us from realizing the possibilities inherent in our lives. We are sometimes afraid to question the validity of new ways of looking at ourselves. Free your mind of these fears and be sensitive to everything around you. Start with no preconceived ideas and explore all the alternatives available to you. Only when you suspend judgment can you embark on the process of creative thinking.

So many new aspects of life will become apparent once you are willing to expand your capacity to think creatively. Investigate what you discover about yourself and your relationships, past and present. Take the knowledge which comes from this increased awareness of your reality and make it work to your advantage. You are the best judge of your present situation.

At this time you are in search of the truth about yourself. Uncovering this truth will involve the courage on your part to look at your separation realistically and to apply your thinking skills toward the resolution of your dilemma. This goal is clearly within your reach. Your willingness to examine every aspect of the alternatives before you is what will lead you in new directions.

By placing the meaning of your experiences in proper perspective you can go on to empower yourself. This will be accomplished by observing carefully the way in which you think.

Exercise

Take time to observe the ways of your own mind and how your mind works. Reinforce useful existing beliefs and create new beliefs that will help you to make new choices.

Fear

When I can read my title clear
To mansions in the skies,
I bid farewell to every fear,
And wipe my weeping eyes.

Isaac Watts

In this period of change you are living through you owe it to
yourself to remove from your path all obstacles which might
prevent you from realizing the new goals you have set for yourself. Fear is one of the greatest impediments to self-realization.
And the fear of loneliness is one of the first emotions to be
conquered during a time of separation, since it gives birth to a
multitude of other fears which can only hinder your progress.
You need to understand the nature of fear in order to overcome
it. The anxiety you are feeling is rooted in a set of beliefs which
are faulty.

One of these mistaken beliefs is that you are incapable of being
alone, even for a limited period of time, and that to do so will
render you helpless. While it is true that you must confront and
understand your fears on your own in order to do away with
them, this should not be equated with loneliness. Think of this
period as one in which you are allowing yourself the freedom to
come to terms with your own reality. This is the time when you
must discover your erroneous beliefs and change them, so that
they will no longer stand in your way. It is only by converting this

fear into something positive that you can truly prevent the separation that fear creates between you and your own true feelings, thoughts and identity.

Fear also feeds upon another illogical belief at a time such as this: the belief that you do not love well enough. Simply stop for a moment and think of the qualities you possess for creating and maintaining meaningful interpersonal relationships and you will see that this fear, like so many, is imaginary. Think of the risks you run if you allow unrealistic fears to block your determination to see your way through this separation with a sense of self-love and a vision of the achievements which lie ahead of you.

Confront those fears which do have true substance. Look at them honestly and determine the course of action within your power for resolving them. These fears should be thought of as a challenge which you are more than prepared to meet.

The overwhelming majority of your preoccupations, however, have no real substance at all. They are the result of faulty beliefs. They are fears which have grown out of your unwillingness to accept your own strength and personal worth. Release yourself from them. Focus on your present reality. Love yourself. Place yourself in harmony with the core of your own spiritual strength and with your capacity to enrich your own life and the lives of others.

In order to discover what is true, what is your destiny, you must demand freedom from all fears.

Exercise

Identify the origins of your fears. Use whatever methods work for you for confronting the realities, and for freeing yourself from the faulty beliefs. Keep foremost in your mind your ability to conquer these fears.

Moment to Moment

Hold every moment sacred. Give each clarity
and meaning, each the weight of thine awareness,
each its true and due fulfillment.

Thomas Mann

Given the pain which you are now going through because of
your separation from a loved one, there is a temptation to allow
the mind to wander back into the negativity of recent past
experiences. Overcome the temptation by insisting on centering
yourself in the present. Seize the moment. If you allow this
precious moment to slip by without appreciating it as part of
the continuity of your life, then it will simply be added to the
past, without ever having been truly lived. And it will be futile
for you to attempt to take hold of it tomorrow. Now is the time
to shape and develop this moment in a meaningful way. Only
the present exists. And it belongs to you.

Immerse yourself totally in whatever your present activity
involves. Keep your active participation in current projects
foremost in your mind. Appreciate the value of what you are
doing. The ultimate merit of your present endeavors lies in
your ability to be the master of your thoughts and actions.

Every small step leads you to the achievement of great
distances. Allow each step in your journey to be recognized for
the immediate value which it represents. The more you are able
to accept every moment of your existence, the more beautiful

will be the outcome of the journey of all your moments as they become days, months and years. Self-awareness is not something which you are planning; it is a force which you are living from moment to moment. And your relationship to the rest of the world is grounded in your present frame of mind. The awareness you will need in order to move ahead is being formulated and reinforced at this very instant.

This is the moment which truly counts. Accept yourself in this moment for everything positive which you represent. And make this attitude a way of life. Your strength is drawn from the past and from your plans for the future. This strength can be validated, however, only in the present. Its continuity depends upon your decision to recognize that this is true.

You live in the here and now. Look around you and absorb what you see, understanding that the reality which surrounds you now is your essential field of action. It is true that your past is incorporated into the way in which you see your present. And the future gives you inspiration for what you are now doing. The fact remains, however, that this very moment represents the totality of your accumulated experiences and your future aspirations.

Exercise

Relax. Take a few deep breaths. Close your eyes. To yourself affirm: "I will concentrate my energies on the present alone and develop my life from moment to moment."

Freedom

What other liberty is there worth having,
if we have not freedom and peace in our minds?

H. D. Thoreau

One of the fundamental necessities for growth is freedom.
Give yourself and the person from whom you are now separating
permission to be free. It is clear that in the development of any
healthy human relationship the mutual giving of freedom is
essential. This period of separation which you are experiencing
is an extension of the relationship itself. Freedom is just as
important in this phase of separation as it was at any other stage
in your association. By choosing freedom for yourself and the
other person, you allow the door to be opened to a world of
possibilities awaiting both of you. It would be unreasonable
to prevent this opening in any way. Why deny yourself or others
this opportunity?

To continue to dwell upon the bonds and restrictions which
once may have defined, in part, your relationship would be to
force yourself to remain in the field of negativity. Now it is
important to see that what the two of you really owe to one
another is a willingness to allow the other person to pursue
life's challenges according to his or her own vision. You
understand that everyone has the right to follow an individual
plan for discovery and development, a plan unhampered by

outside resistance. Take it upon yourself to put this understanding into action. Begin to live as a free person, allowing the other person to do the same. Ultimately, you are bound to yourself and to a greater Power which unifies all the aspirations of mankind. When all of your commitments in life are seen in this light, freedom comes more easily.

The giving and taking of freedom is certainly one of the most difficult challenges with which you will be faced during this time of separation. It is natural to want to cling to what we already understand or think we understand. This clinging may give you a sense of security. But it is a false sense of security, one which can only prevent you and the other person from getting on with the business of the rest of life. Letting go demands freedom.

What lies ahead of you is nothing less than the infinite possibility of choices. As you look toward your future, you see before you ways which can lead you to your own greater development. Feel free to follow them.

Exercise

Ask yourself what aspects of your personality or circumstances are holding you back from experiencing personal freedom. Write down your impressions of what these negative forces might be. Write freely. Do not analyze what you are writing. Just let the words flow. When you feel the need, repeat this exercise until you can honestly say to yourself, "I am free."

This book was designed with two primary goals
in mind: the growth of your self-knowledge
and the development of your ability to act in a
way that is beneficial to you. It is sincerely
hoped that these goals have been met, that
The Art of Letting Go has helped you to work
through the difficulties of a breakup in a
relationship. You should allow at least 21 days
of conscientiously practicing the exercises
which accompany each unit. At this point you
will begin to see clearly the positive results of
your endeavors. I welcome your comments and
wish you well on your journey.

Carlino Giampolo
P.O. Box 15182
Honolulu, Hawaii 96815

Notes